Anne,

Thankyou for doing my da[...]
[...]e & wishing you lots of [...]
the future.

With love,

Sue Hennessy.

Your Book of Ballet

The YOUR BOOK Series

Acting
Aeromodelling
Animal Drawing
Aquaria
Astronomy
Badminton
Ballet
Bridges
Butterflies and Moths
Cake Making and
 Decorating
Camping
The Way a Car Works
Card Games
Card Tricks
Chemistry
Chess
Coin Collecting
Computers
Confirmation
Contract Bridge
Medieval and Tudor
 Costume
Seventeenth and Eighteenth
 Century Costume
Nineteenth Century Costume
Cricket
Dinghy Sailing
The Earth
Electronics
Embroidery
Engines and Turbines
Fencing
Film-making
Fishes
Flower Arranging

Flower Making
Flying
Freshwater Life
Golf
Gymnastics
Hovercraft
The Human Body
Judo
Kites
Knitted Toys
Knitting and Crochet
Knots
Landscape Drawing
Light
Magic
Maps and Map Reading
Mental Magic
Model Car Racing
Modelling
Money
Music
Paper Folding
Parliament
Party Games
Patchwork
Patience
Pet Keeping
Photography
Photographing Wild Life
Keeping Ponies
Prehistoric Britain
Puppetry
The Recorder
Roman Britain
Rugger

Sea Fishing
The Seashore
Self-Defence
Sewing
Shell Collecting
Skating
Soccer
Sound
Space Travel
Squash
Stamps
Surnames
Swimming
Survival Swimming and
 Life Saving
Swimming Games and
 Activities
Table Tennis
Table Tricks
Tape Recording
Television
Tennis
Trampolining
Trees
Veteran and Edwardian Cars
Vintage Cars
Watching Wild Life
Waterways
The Weather
Woodwork

YOUR BOOK OF

BALLET

Peter L. Moldon

FABER & FABER
3 Queen Square London

First published in 1974
by Faber and Faber Limited
3 Queen Square London WC1
Printed in Great Britain by
Latimer Trend & Company Ltd Plymouth

ISBN 0 571 10241 7

To the memory of my father

Contents

Acknowledgements	*page* 13
1. What is Ballet?	15
2. History	25
3. Technique	36
4. A Dancer's Day	45
5. Taking up Ballet	51
6. British Ballet Today	54
7. Ballet on the Screen	66
Reading List	69
Index	73

Illustrations

Plates

1. Lancret's painting of Camargo   *facing page* 32
2. Chalon's lithograph of Taglioni in *La Sylphide*   32
3. Pavlova in *The Dying Swan*   33
4. Nijinsky in *Le Spectre de la Rose*   33
5. Vladimir Vasiliev in *Spartacus*   48
6. A young student practising mime   *after page* 48
7. Julia Farron teaching the Lilac Fairy's mime   48
8. A classical class   48
9. A Graham class   48
10. Nadia Nerina and David Blair in *La Fille mal gardée*
    facing page 49
11. Margot Fonteyn in *The Sleeping Beauty*   54
12. *Symphonic Variations*   55
13. *The Grand Tour*   55
14. *The Three Cornered Hat*   58
15. Scottish Theatre Ballet's *Giselle*   58
16. *Peter and the Wolf*   59

17. Christopher Bruce in *Pierrot Lunaire*   *facing page* 59

18. *Ziggurat*   64

19. *Three Epitaphs*   65

20. Norman McLaren's film *Pas de Deux*   65

Line drawings

Olga Spessivtseva and Serge Lifar in Diaghilev's Russian
Ballet *Swan Lake*   *half title page*

Vazira Ganibalova of the Kirov in a typical Russian split
jeté   *title page*

The auditorium at Covent Garden   *page* 14

The development of the ballet dress   29

The five positions of the feet   36

Svetlana Beriosova in an *arabesque*   37

Yuri Soloviev in an *attitude*   38

André Prokovsky in a *cabriole*   39

Erik Bruhn performing *entrechats*   40

Vladimir Vasiliev in a *grand jeté*   41

Antoinette Sibley turning during a *pirouette*   42

Men of the Kirov Ballet in class   47

Ekaterina Maximova at a rehearsal   48

The photograph on the front cover shows Julia
Blaikie and Leigh Warren in Ballet Rambert's *There
Was a Time*; those on the back cover Rudolf Nureyev
in *Le Corsaire* and Tamara Karsavina in *Carnaval*

Acknowledgements

I would like to thank all those who have helped to make this book possible: the various ballet companies who have been unstinting in their help and have allowed me to watch class and rehearsals; Michael Wood, Director of the Royal Ballet School, and the dancers and friends who have read part or all of the manuscript or proofs and made valuable comments. I am grateful to the following for permitting me to reproduce their photographs: The Trustees of the Wallace Collection (Plate 1); The National Film Board of Canada (20); Anthony Crickmay (8, 14, 17 and back cover—Nureyev); Alan Cunliffe (18 and front cover); Mike Davis (19); Zoë Dominic (13); Bob Johnson (15); Helen Leoussi (9); Roger PIC (5); Houston Rogers (10 and 11); Leslie Spatt (12) and Jennie Walton (6, 7 and 16). I would also like to thank the *Dancing Times* Picture Library for the loan of the print for Plate 8 and Jennie Walton for allowing me to borrow from her collection the photograph of Karsavina reproduced on the back cover.

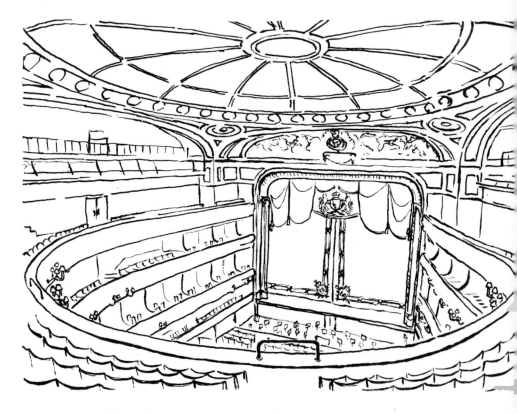

The auditorium at Covent Garden seen from the amphitheatre

1. *What is Ballet?*

Introduction

Imagine that you are inside the Royal Opera House, Covent Garden. You are settled in your red plush seat. You look around at the horseshoe-shaped auditorium, with electric candelabra and ornamental figures lining each tier. The box next but one to the stage on the middle level—the Grand Tier—is pointed out to you. It is the Royal Box. And, because it is the *Royal* Opera House, you will see the Royal Family's coat of arms on the pelmet of the stage curtain and the monogram of Queen Elizabeth II embroidered in gold on both halves of the heavy red velvet curtain.

The lights dim. A hush comes over the audience. The conductor comes out on to the rostrum and acknowledges the applause. He turns to the musicians and raises his baton. The orchestra begins to play. The curtain rises with a barely audible swish. The ballet has begun.

However, before continuing this flight of fancy, let us first consider: What is ballet? Ballet is just one aspect of what is known as the dance. Dance is many things. It is primitive man, splendidly arrayed in feathers and war paint, dancing round a fire in the middle of the jungle. It is English Morris dancers on the village green. It is elegant couples—the girls in long ball dresses, the men in white tie and tails—waltzing round a ballroom. It is teenagers in a *discothèque* dancing to the latest record in the Top Twenty. Yet none of these are ballet. Apart from anything else, ballet is a dance form that needs an audience.

But I expect you already have an image of what the word means to you. Is it, perhaps, dancers dressed in long white skirts, skimming silently across a moonlight flooded stage? Well, if that is so, then you are right. That is ballet. But it is only one type of ballet. As you read the rest of this book you will discover that ballet is many other things as well, some so far removed from this romantic image that they may seem to exist in another art and another world.

The romantic ballet I have just mentioned has certain things which are common to every ballet. First and foremost, it has dancers. Secondly, someone has arranged the dances. He or she is known as the choreographer. Thirdly, the dancers dance to some accompaniment: the music. Finally, the dancers wear costumes and dance in a suitable setting: this is design.

Now let us take a look at each of these four elements in a little more detail.

The Dancer

Without the dancer there would be no ballet. It would be possible to do away with all the other elements, letting the dancers improvise their movements in silence without benefit of setting or costumes, and there would still be a ballet. But as a general rule dancers are in the hands of the choreographer, who moulds them into the movements and patterns decided on by him.

The success of a ballet depends on the aptitude that the dancers show for interpreting the choreographer's wishes. If the dancers are not capable of performing the steps devised by the choreographer or bringing to life the characters that he wishes to show, then the ballet will fail. So, dancers must have a fine command of technique, the vocabulary of the dance. This technique should look easy, not difficult or impossible to perform. So, first and foremost, a dancer must be in perfect control of his body, able to make each and every part do his bidding. However, technique is not enough. It is only a means to an end, the end being expression. The most perfect technique in the world will seem as nothing without expression.

A dancer must be able to characterise. The ability to act through movement is very important. It may be through the old-fashioned mime of classical ballets, such as *Swan Lake* and *The Sleeping Beauty*, where communication is by means of certain set gestures of the hands and arms. Or it may be through a more naturalistic, yet still theatrical, style of acting, such as that seen in the role of Juliet. At times passages of a ballet can seem like a silent play set to music, yet the emotional power of such episodes should not be underestimated.

There are three distinct kinds of dancer, though it should be pointed out that not every dancer fits into these categories. Firstly, there is the purely classical dancer. He or she will, in time, come to dance the leading roles in classical ballets, as well as in the more recent works in the classical technique.

The best known of these is the ballerina. The ballerina is born not made. She has a quality which immediately distinguishes her from the other dancers on stage. The term ballerina is often applied indiscriminately to almost any female dancer who has danced a few solo or principal roles, but in truth, there are generally barely a dozen throughout the world at any one time. At present two of the most famous ballerinas are Margot Fonteyn and the Bolshoi Ballet's Maya Plisetskaya.

Even rarer than the ballerina is the male counterpart, the *danseur noble*. He is born to appear as the princes of ballet and to partner the ballerina. He moves with grace and nobility, dances with style and shows his partner off to the best advantage. Fonteyn's former partner Michael Somes was a *danseur noble* and so is Plisetskaya's partner Nikolai Fadeyechev.

At the other extreme from the classical dancer is the character dancer. As the name implies the dancer appears in the character roles in ballet, where the miming of the part is more important than the dancing and the dancer's features are hidden by an exaggerated make-up. He or she will also appear in the national dances in ballets such as *Swan Lake* or *Coppélia*.

Between the two extremes of classical and character dancer comes the *demi-caractère* dancer. This dancer is difficult to define, but easy enough to pick out on stage. The *demi-caractère* dancer generally portrays a more positive character and dances more brilliantly than the classical dancer. Indeed, the *demi-caractère* dancer will be physically or temperamentally unsuited to the big classical roles, although he or she may still be expected to appear in them. It is a curious fact that most of the great male dancers of this century, from Nijinsky to Nureyev, Soloviev and Vasiliev, have been *demi-caractère* dancers.

In addition to the soloists and principals, any large classical ballet company will also have a *corps de ballet*. These dancers generally perform the same steps in unison, forming into the group patterns devised by the choreographer. The female *corps* is seen at its most poetic in ballet classics such as *Giselle* and *Swan Lake*.

The Choreographer

The choreographer is the person who creates the actual dances which make up a ballet. The ballet begins with him. Either he has an idea which he feels will make a suitable ballet or he feels inspired to create dances to a particular piece of music. The length of the music will determine whether the ballet will be in one, two, three or even four acts. Most probably it will be in only one act, as it is extremely difficult to sustain an idea or a plot for longer than this.

There are two distinct types of ballet: narrative, and abstract, which is pure dance without any story element. Strictly, there can be no such thing as a completely abstract ballet, as a ballet uses dancers, and dancers are not dancing machines but people, who, intentionally or otherwise, generate a mood or emotion in addition to that produced by the dance patterns.

Of course, some ballets fall between the plotless and the narrative, where a slight plot or theme may be apparent without being crucial to the ballet. A good example of this is Jerome Robbins' *Dances at a Gathering*. The dancers do not portray specific characters and there is no story as such, yet there is the feeling of people in the open air on a hot summer's day. There are meetings, partings; couples pair off for a while; there is humour, joy and sadness.

Ballet can convey these subtle and fleeting expressions of feeling so much better than any words. However, situations that would normally rely on words are difficult to convey in ballet. For instance, a choreographer cannot arrange a long 'conversation' betweeen his dancers except through long-winded mime. Similarly, he cannot indicate that one person is the father-in-law of another, or that a character is forty-seven years old—except through a programme note.

Dancers are people, and they will probably influence the choreographer as he works on his ballet. Indeed, the best ballets are often those which bring out the particular qualities of the dancers used. But not all choreographers work in this way. Rather than seek inspiration from the dancers, they prefer to map out the entire ballet before attending the first rehearsal. Who is to say which method is the better?

The choreographer is not only responsible for creating the dances. He must also choose the music, the dancers and the designer. In other words, the choreographer is usually the master-mind behind the ballet, and it is up to him to create something that works as a total conception.

The Music

Music is an integral part of ballet. It produces the rhythms for the dancers and the emotional power for the audience. It can range from the earliest pre-classical music to the most *avant-garde* electronic score. Music which already exists may inspire the choreographer to choose his theme and dance patterns; but many of the best ballets have music specially written for them. Then, if necessary, the choreographer can stipulate the length of the work and the mood at any given moment.

However, it is an expensive business to commission a composer to write a ballet score, so most of the time a choreographer will use existing music. Unfortunately this can produce all sorts of complications. The choreographer will find himself with a climax coming in the wrong place, too much music where he doesn't need it or too little where he does. The resulting ballet can rarely be completely satisfactory.

Ballet is a silent art, the dancers moving in time and space to music without ever uttering a word. Well, hardly ever. There are a few exceptions, particularly in modern ballet, where the dancers do break into speech. For instance, there is Naomi Lapzeson's *Cantabile* (for London Contemporary Dance Theatre) and Anna Sokolow's *Opus '65* (Ballet Rambert) where the dancers speak, but the words are barely distinguishable. Robert North's *Brian* (London Contemporary Dance) has two of the dancers talking most of the time. Even Frederick Ashton's classical *La Fille mal gardée* has everyone singing 'La, la, la' as they dance off at the very end. But generally the dancers stay silent.

This doesn't stop the accompaniment to a ballet being either speech or song. For example, the voices of two couples form the background to Christopher Bruce's *Living Space* (Ballet Rambert) and Frank Staff's *Peter and the Wolf* (see page 62) has a narrator and orchestra. There are two singers in Kenneth MacMillan's ballet to Mahler's *Song of the Earth* and singers galore—and four grand pianos too—in Bronislava Nijinska's ballet to Stravinsky's *Les Noces* (both in the Royal Ballet repertory).

Ballets are even given without any music at all. Christopher Bruce's *For these who die as cattle* (Ballet Rambert) is an example. And sometimes passages of a ballet are danced without music, as is the case in *Living Space* and several of the ballets of Glen Tetley.

Design

The designer is usually an artist. There have been many famous artists who have designed for the ballet, such as Chagall and Picasso. However, the stage designer's job is a specialised art which requires a practical knowledge of the theatre. It is not simply a matter of creating an appropriate and attractive stage picture. There are many other things that ought to be taken into account.

Dancers must be visible. They should have sufficient floor space on which to dance. The setting has to be seen from all parts of the theatre.

Effective design creates atmosphere. If the ballet is plotless the designer should complement what the choreographer is trying to do with the dancers and the music, and help to create the mood by the use of colour and form. In a narrative ballet the designer creates characters with his costumes. There is all the difference in the world between the costume worn by a prince and a beggar. It is not only the shape and patterns, but also the quality of the material which will be different. If the costume is right then it will help the dancer in the creation of the character he or she has to portray. In a dancing role the costume should also show off the line of the dancer's body and allow him to move freely, but in a role requiring no dancing this is not so important.

Lighting

Lighting is a highly specialized subject, quite separate from design. However, as it is so closely allied to design, I have included it under the same heading.

The audience is probably unaware of most of the changes that take place in the lighting during the performance of any ballet. They will notice the spotlights following the principals, but that is all. In fact the light changes frequently in intensity and colour in accordance with the mood of any given dance or series of dances.

As with design the lighting should make the dancers visible. Far too often dancers become almost invisible under murky lighting. The lighting man will probably reply to any complaint by saying that he is creating mood and atmosphere, but this shouldn't be at the expense of visibility.

Stage lighting has improved so much in recent years that it has become possible to dispense with settings altogether and rely entirely on lighting to achieve the desired effect. This occurs more often in modern dance, where painted scenery tends to look out of place.

Conclusions

So, those are the four elements which go into the making of any ballet. If they are all on an equally high level then it should be a very fine ballet. However, masterpieces are rare. Nevertheless you can get great pleasure from the less than perfect ballet. Indeed, items that have only fine dancing to recommend them can be completely enjoyable. I am thinking in particular of the concert items so beloved of Russian dancers, which for sheer enjoyment could hardly be bettered. Apart from the familiar extracts from the classics, you will see items specially devised for concert perform-ances. These will probably include an exciting solo for a male character dancer wearing traditional Russian costume; a so-called 'lift and drift' number—a romantic piece in which the woman, dressed in flimsiest chiffon, is carried aloft by the man; and an acrobatic duet in which the woman does death-defying dives into her partner's arms. There will be no setting, the costumes will probably be embarrassingly bad, the choreography banal, the music trite, yet the artistry of the dancers can lift the pieces above their mundane components into something sublime.

You the Audience

Let us now return to that imaginary visit to Covent Garden. How are you going to get the most out of the performance? Read the programme and find out all you need to know about the ballet or ballets that you'll be seeing. If you don't possess opera glasses and want to use those belonging to the theatre, get them out before the ballet starts. Sitting still will aid your concentration. Sit back and try to take in as much as you can. Watch and listen. Concentrate on the ballerina, but not to the exclusion of everyone else. But, most important of all: relax and enjoy yourself.

One occasion which is particularly enjoyable and exciting is a Gala performance. Generally this will take place in the presence of at least one member of the Royal Family. The audience will look its glittering best, with the women in long evening gowns and the men in dinner suits. On stage probably there will be the *première* of some new and talked-of ballet, and the principals of the company will be seen in show-stopping 'party' pieces.

However, be warned. Ballet-going is like a disease: once it gets into the blood you won't get rid of it. It starts harmlessly with one performance here and one there. Gradually you'll see more ballets, more companies, more performances of the same ballet with different casts. It will soon take up all your money and all your time. You'll start to eat, drink, sleep and think ballet. Your non-ballet-minded friends will think you've gone mad. But you won't care. You'll be in seventh heaven.

2. *History*

Court Ballet

It is difficult to state exactly how and when ballet began. But to all intents and purposes it can be said to have started with the court ballets of the sixteenth century.

Catherine de' Medici, the wife of the French king Henri II, was responsible for introducing ballet to the French court. The most famous ballet of her time was a sumptuous entertainment in 1581 known as the *Ballet Comique de la Reine* (*Ballet* meaning here 'a geometric combination of several persons dancing together') which celebrated in song, dance and verse the wedding of the Queen's sister to the Duc de Joyeuse. The ballet told the story of the enchantress Circe. The action took place on the floor of a great hall, with the spectators seated on three sides.

Court ballet reached its peak during the reign of Louis XIV. Like the two previous French monarchs, Louis danced in the ballets, generally appearing as a god or some other exalted creature. He gained the name *Le Roi Soleil* (The Sun King) from his part as the Sun in *Le Ballet Royal de la Nuit* (*The Royal Ballet of the Night*). When Louis gave up dancing ballet passed from the court to the public stage.

Camargo

In the beginning women's parts were taken by men. The first professional female dancers made their appearance in 1681 in a ballet called *Le Triomphe de l'Amour* (*The Triumph of Love*). The first really famous dancer was Marie-Anne Cupis de Camargo, and she was celebrated for her technique. Her only serious rival was Marie Sallé. In 1730 Camargo created a sensation when she shortened her long skirt by several inches to enable her to perform simple jumps and beaten steps. (The picture opposite page 32 shows Camargo in her shortened costume.) Incidentally, since the early court ballets the costume for male dancers had been based on that for an officer of ancient Rome.

Noverre and Vestris

Jean Georges Noverre was a choreographer of note. Perhaps his finest achievement was to replace the series of conventional dances which then made up a ballet with the ballet of action, in which dance and story were united. His theory behind the *ballet d'action*, together with many other suggestions for ballet reform, were contained in his famous *Letters on the Dance*. Although they were published in 1760, his principles are as valid now as they were in his day.

The year 1760 also saw the birth of one of the most famous dancers in the history of ballet, Auguste Vestris, who was renowned for the extraordinary height of his jumps. There is an amusing story told about Vestris. A woman who had accidentally trodden on his toe apologized and asked if she had hurt him.

'No, madam,' he replied, 'but you have almost put all Paris in mourning for a fortnight.'

The Romantic Ballet

The origins of the romantic movement were literary: its sources of inspiration included the occult and the supernatural. The movement spread to painting, music and, inevitably, to ballet. The first completely romantic ballet was *La Sylphide*, premièred in 1832 with choreography by Filippo Taglioni. It told the story of the sylphide, a supernatural creature who fell in love with a mortal. The role of the sylphide was created by the choreographer's daughter, Marie Taglioni, the dancer most closely associated with the romantic ballet. For the part she wore a tight fitting bodice which left her neck and shoulders free, a white muslin skirt, pale pink tights and satin shoes. This became the accepted costume for the romantic ballet. It gave this ballerina greater freedom of movement than had been possible before and allowed her to jump high into the air. Dancing on the tips of the toes (on *pointe*), which had been introduced some years before, enhanced the ballerina's lightness. The air had become the romantic ballerina's natural element.

Giselle

La Sylphide was the first of many ballets featuring strange and mysterious creatures such as ondines, peris and *wilis*. *Wilis* were spirits of girls who died before their wedding day and they appeared in *Giselle*, the undoubted masterpiece of the romantic era. This ballet was first given in Paris in 1841 with Carlotta Grisi in the title role. The music was by Adolphe Adam and the choreography by Jean Corelli and Jules Perrot, who had been a pupil of Vestris and a partner of Taglioni.

Giselle is a peasant girl who falls in love with a young man known to her as Loys. When she discovers that Loys is no peasant but Prince Albrecht in disguise and that he is engaged to someone else, she goes mad and dies of a broken heart.

The second act of the ballet is set in the forest where Giselle is buried. She is summoned from her grave by Myrthe, Queen of the *wilis*. Albrecht comes to lay flowers at Giselle's grave and Myrthe commands Albrecht to dance to the point of exhaustion. Giselle's love for Albrecht saves him from death and, as dawn breaks, the *wilis* return to their graves leaving Albrecht alone.

As I am sure you are aware, *Giselle* is still performed to this day. The dancer portraying Giselle has a remarkable and demanding role in which both acting and dancing must be on an equally high level: the mad scene requiring great dramatic gifts and the second act lightness and elevation. Indeed, this second act can become a dance poem of unmatchable beauty: a fitting legacy from the romantic ballet.

Petipa and the Classical Ballet

By the middle of the nineteenth century ballet in Europe had gone into a decline, and it is to Russia that we must look for the next important phase in the history of ballet.

Russia had had a state ballet school since 1735, so it is not surprising that dancers, choreographers and musicians were drawn to a country where ballet had such a fine tradition. Amongst these artists was the Frenchman Marius Petipa, who came to St Petersburg to be principal dancer. In the course of his dancing career he partnered Fanny Elssler, one of the most celebrated ballerinas of the romantic era, during her tour of Russia.

However, Petipa's importance lies in the ballets that he choreographed. During his long career he created numerous ballets, many in four or five acts. His main object was to show off the ballerina and soloists to the best advantage, using the *corps de ballet* generally as a decorative background. The story was told through the elaborate sign language of mime. One act was usually given over to a series of unrelated dances or *divertissements*. The highlight of these was the *pas de deux* for the two principals. This opened with an *adage* for the ballerina and her partner in which the ballerina's line (a pleasing and flowing arrangement of her arms, head, body and legs) and balance were displayed. Sometimes the *corps* accompanied the principals in the *adage*. This was followed by a solo (also known as a variation) for the man, and another for the ballerina, each showing their technical brilliance, and the *pas de deux* concluded with a fast and exciting *coda*. I should mention that the ballerina's costume by this time was the now familiar *tutu*, though the skirt then was longer and wider than that in use today.

The development of the ballet dress
(*Left*) The romantic ballet skirt; (*centre*) the *tutu* at the end of the nineteenth century; (*right*) the *tutu* today

Petipa's most famous ballets are probably *La Bayadère, Raymonda* (the last acts of these can still be seen in the Royal Ballet's repertory in versions mounted by Rudolf Nureyev) and *The Sleeping Beauty*.

The Sleeping Beauty

This ballet is generally considered to be Petipa's masterwork. It was given its first performance at the Maryinsky Theatre, St Petersburg (now Leningrad) in 1890. Tchaikovsky's music for *The Sleeping Beauty* abounds in memorable themes and is eminently danceable. As a ballet composer Tchaikovsky has never been equalled, except, perhaps, in this century by Stravinsky.

The Sleeping Beauty is a ballet in four acts, or, to be strictly accurate, a prologue and three acts. It tells the familiar story of Princess Aurora, woken by a Prince's kiss from a hundred years' sleep. In the prologue there are a number of brilliant solos for the fairies attending Aurora's christening. The first act takes place sixteen years later. It contains one of the most famous dances in all ballet, the Rose Adagio, for Aurora and her four princely suitors. The next act, generally known as the Vision scene, takes place one hundred years later and is a poetic encounter between Prince Florimund and a vision of the beautiful Aurora. The last act, in true Petipa style, is a *divertissement*. Various fairy tale characters are present at the wedding of Aurora and Florimund, including Puss in Boots and the White Cat, and the fluttering Bluebird and his Princess. The ballet culminates in the *Grand pas de deux* for Aurora and Florimund.

The Sleeping Beauty is a magical story told with the aid of sumptuous sets and costumes, lavish group dances, sparkling solos and beautiful duets to the accompaniment of some of Tchaikovsky's most inspired music. No wonder it has survived to this very day in the repertory of nearly every large ballet company.

Ivanov

Lev Ivanov became assistant ballet master at the Maryinsky after retiring as a dancer. His first major assignment was to take over from the sick Petipa as choreographer of *The Nutcracker*. However, Ivanov's importance rests on another Tchaikovsky ballet, *Swan Lake*.

Swan Lake

The first version of the ballet, given in Moscow in 1877 with choreography by Reisinger, had been an artistic disaster. Subsequent productions fared little better until the second act was given with choreography by Ivanov at the Maryinsky in 1894 at a concert to honour the memory of the composer, who had died four months previously. The complete ballet was given the following year, with choreography for acts two and four by Ivanov and by Petipa for the other two acts. It is Ivanov's choreography, particularly of act two, that has ensured the ballet's lasting success. In recent years many choreographers have attempted new versions of the ballet but most have wisely left Ivanov's sublime second act intact.

Although *Swan Lake* is purely classical in technique it has a very romantic story. This tells of Prince Siegfried's love for Odette, an enchanted Princess. During the day she and her friends are transformed by the evil magician von Rothbart into swans; only at night do they resume their human form. Odette's and Siegfried's love is expressed in a lyrical *pas de deux* which is the heart of Ivanov's second act.

However, von Rothbart brings his daughter Odile to the ball celebrating Siegfried's coming of age. Odile looks just like Odette—not surprisingly, as the same dancer usually performs both roles—and Siegfried believes that she is really Odette. In a sparkling and brilliant duet, known as the Black Swan *pas de deux*, Odile succeeds in captivating Siegfried. He vows to marry Odile, discovering too late that he has been tricked. He rushes back to Odette at the lakeside and together they commit suicide. The magician's power is broken, he dies, and the swans resume their human form. Siegfried and Odette are united for evermore beneath the waters of the lake.

Fokine

Michel Fokine can be considered as the father of twentieth-century ballet. At the beginning of the century he was dancer, ballet master and choreographer at the Maryinsky. Like Noverre before him, Fokine was a reformer. In his ballets Fokine abolished the antiquated mime of the Petipa ballets, did away with the classical *tutus* that were obligatory for every ballet, replacing them with costumes appropriate to the period in which the ballet was set, and forbade the taking of calls during the stage action. His opportunity to instigate further reforms came when Diaghilev took the Russian ballet to Europe with Fokine as choreographer and ballet master.

Diaghilev

Serge Diaghilev was a member of a group of young men who had a considerable effect on Russian art. Diaghilev staged art exhibitions, edited a magazine called *World of Art* and for a time was employed by the Imperial Theatres, which were all under the direct control of the Tsar. Yet Diaghilev was not an artist, nor was he a dancer or choreographer—though he was quite a good amateur singer! No, his genius lay in discovering and bringing out the talent in others. He was a sort of glorified impresario, one of his achievements being to bring Russian art, music, ballet and opera to Europe.

A detail from
Lancret's painting of Camargo

Chalon's lithograph
of Marie Taglioni
in the second act
of *La Sylphide*

Anna Pavlova
in *The Dying Swan*

Vaslav Nijinsky
in *Le Spectre de la Rose*

During the first Paris season of opera and ballet in 1909 the Fokine works presented included *Le Pavillon d'Armide* and *Les Sylphides* (not to be confused with *La Sylphide*). The company was a tremendous success and Tamara Karsavina, Anna Pavlova and Vaslav Nijinsky leaped to fame. This was to be the only season when Pavlova danced for Diaghilev. She was to go on and form her own company, dancing mainly concert numbers in which her great artistry transcended the often banal choreography. The work immortalized by Pavlova was *The Dying Swan*, a solo created for her by Fokine during their Maryinsky days.

The company Diaghilev presented in the West was composed of dancers who were still members of the Maryinsky and the Bolshoi, and so were only free to dance outside Russia during their holidays. He wanted a company that could perform throughout the year, so in 1913 he broke away from the Imperial Theatres and formed his own company. Diaghilev's Russian Ballet became one of the greatest ballet companies the world has ever known.

Its repertory included several other works by Fokine, including *Petrushka*, *The Firebird* and *Le Spectre de la Rose*. The last had only two dancers, Karsavina as a girl dreaming of her first ball and Nijinsky as the spirit of the rose. In his legendary final leap Nijinsky seemed to fly out into the night.

Fokine left the company when Diaghilev made Nijinsky his choreographer. Nijinsky created four ballets: *L'Après-midi d'un faune* (*Afternoon of a Faun*), *Le Sacre du Printemps* (*The Rite of Spring*), *Jeux* (literally *Games*, known in England as *Playtime*) and *Tyl Eulenspiegel*. Nijinsky's primitive choreography and Stravinsky's barbaric score for *Le Sacre du Printemps* created a scandal at the ballet's *première* when the smart Parisian audience hissed, whistled, shouted insults and fought one another.

After Nijinsky left Diaghilev, his place was taken, in turn, by Leonide Massine, Bronislava Nijinska (Nijinsky's sister), George

c

Balanchine and Serge Lifar. The accent was on all that was new in choreography, music and design. However, Diaghilev didn't entirely neglect the classics. In the early years he staged *Giselle* and a condensed, two-act version of *Swan Lake*. In 1921 he presented *The Sleeping Princess* (as he called it) at the Alhambra Theatre in London, but it was a financial disaster. This may seem surprising today, but in the twenties Diaghilev had accustomed his audiences to expect one act novelties rather than what seemed to them dusty period pieces lasting a whole evening.

Ballet Today

Diaghilev died in 1929 and his company died with him. But his influence did not die. His dancers and choreographers dispersed and spread his ideas throughout the western world.

Marie Rambert came to London and formed what became the Ballet Rambert. Her first guest artists were Tamara Karsavina and Leon Woizikowski. At about the same time Ninette de Valois formed the Vic-Wells Ballet, or, as it is now known, the Royal Ballet. Her first ballerina was Alicia Markova. Later Markova and another Diaghilev dancer, Anton Dolin, were to form Festival Ballet. British ballet as we know it today would have been unthinkable without Diaghilev.

In its short life British ballet has already managed to make itself felt abroad. Robert Helpmann and Peggy van Praagh are in charge of the Australian Ballet, Celia Franca of the National Ballet of Canada and David Poole of Capab Ballet in South Africa. Former members of the Royal Ballet have also become ballet directors of some of the European opera houses, including John Field at Milan and the late John Cranko at Stuttgart.

Serge Lifar stayed in Europe and became dancer, ballet master and choreographer at the Paris Opéra. He became the founder of a style of French ballet which led, eventually, to the works of Roland Petit and Maurice Béjart, who today runs a successful company in Brussels.

George Balanchine went to the United States and became director and choreographer of New York City Ballet. In its early years American Ballet Theatre employed many Diaghilev dancers and choreographers, including Markova and Fokine. However, most of America's companies are markedly American in style. The Joffrey Ballet, for instance, could hardly have come from anywhere but America.

However, companies which already had a strong tradition of their own were not greatly affected by Diaghilev. The Royal Danish Ballet in Copenhagen has continued to train dancers in the style of August Bournonville, its great nineteenth-century ballet master and choreographer, though it also performs a wide range of contemporary ballets. In Russia Soviet ballet has developed in its own way since the Revolution. The two major Russian companies are the Bolshoi Ballet in Moscow and the Kirov (formerly the Maryinsky) Ballet in Leningrad. 'Bolshoi' literally means big, and this aptly describes the Moscow company. Its ballets are large-scale and dramatic, its impact immediate. There is no doubt that the Bolshoi is the most exciting ballet company in the world. In contrast, the Kirov is less theatrical; the purity of the dancing being what matters most of all. For sheer elegance and style the Leningrad company is second to none. With two such great companies, no wonder Russia is still the Mecca for ballet lovers the world over.

3. Technique

Classical ballet has a well-defined set of rules. These were formulated in France and account for all those French ballet terms which tend to mystify the beginner.

The three basic demands of classical dancing are correct posture, good flexibility of leg joints, and turnout, in that order of importance—as all who enter for G.C.E. O. Level Ballet will learn. Turnout means that the legs, from the hips downwards, are rotated outwards. Good turnout enhances the line of a dancer, but some lack of it does not prevent a dancer from becoming famous. Equally important is *plié*, which is the bending of the knees. Most movements begin or end with *plié*; without *plié* they would be stiff and stilted.

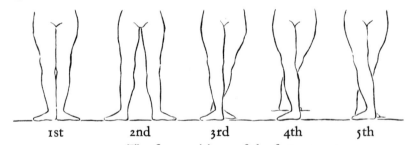

| 1st | 2nd | 3rd | 4th | 5th |

The five positions of the feet
Notice that in 2nd and 4th position the feet are separated from
each other by the distance of approximately one foot

The five positions of the feet, which were developed in the court ballets of Louis XIV, were used to make the dancer appear more elegant. They are the starting point for all steps.

There are also five corresponding positions of the arms, but I will not confuse you by illustrating them as they differ slightly from one teaching system to another. Arm movements are known as *ports de bras*.

It isn't essential to know all the terms used to be able to enjoy ballet, but a knowledge of some of the more familiar will aid your ballet appreciation. Here are a few of them listed alphabetically.

Arabesque

The *arabesque* is one of the basic poses of classical ballet. In this the dancer stands on one leg, the other being extended behind in the air. There are many different types of *arabesque*. In the most familiar one arm continues the line of the raised leg.

Svetlana Beriosova
of the Royal Ballet
in an *arabesque*

Attitude

The *attitude* was inspired by the famous statue of the Flying Mercury by Giovanni da Bologna. In this pose the supporting leg can be straight or bent, with the raised leg bent behind and one arm raised to echo the curve of this leg. The leg in the air can also be raised to the front.

Yuri Soloviev of the Kirov Ballet in an heroic *attitude*

Bourrée sur les pointes

In this the dancer advances in a series of tiny steps which give the impression of gliding across the stage. You can look for *bourrées* in the first solo of the Queen of the *wilis* in *Giselle*.

Cabriole

This step is a jump in which the lower leg rises to beat against the other while the dancer is in mid air.

André Prokovsky in a *cabriole*

Entrechat

In this step the dancer rises in the air, crossing and uncrossing the legs several times. Nijinsky was supposed to be able to perform the phenomenal *entrechat dix*, which entails five beats of the legs while the dancer is in the air.

Erik Bruhn, Danish born and trained, performing *entrechats*. He is wearing a kilt for Bournonville's *La Sylphide*, set in Scotland

Fouetté

Fouettés (strictly, *fouettés ronds de jambe en tournant*) are performed on point using a whipping movement of the working leg, which causes the dancer to turn. It is almost exclusively a female step. The most famous *fouettés* are the thirty-two in the *coda* to the Black Swan *pas de deux* in traditional versions of *Swan Lake*.

The *fouetté* was introduced into Russia in 1893 by the Italian ballerina Pierina Legnani in *Cinderella*. On that first occasion the teenage Fokine was on stage as a pageboy. He got so carried away by Legnani's thirty-two *fouettés* that he forgot where he was and applauded. Not surprisingly he was severely reprimanded.

Jeté

A *jeté* is a jump from one leg on to the other. The most familiar is the *grand jeté*, in which the dancer leaps high into the air—generally to gasps from the audience.

Vladimir Vasiliev of the Bolshoi Ballet in a *grand jeté*

Pirouette

The *pirouette* is a turning movement on one leg. Considerable speed can be achieved in *pirouettes* and they can be very exciting to watch.

Antoinette Sibley of the Royal Ballet turning during a *pirouette*

Tour en l'air

In this the dancer rises vertically and turns in the air before landing. The *double tour en l'air*, in which the dancer does two complete turns in the air, is almost exclusively a male step. It is performed three times successively by Siegfried in most versions of his solo in the Black Swan *pas de deux*.

Modern Dance

So far I have dealt only with classical ballet. However, new ballet techniques and style have evolved during this century. These are known as modern dance. There have been many creators of modern dance, particularly in America and Germany, but I have space to tell you about only one of these, the American Martha Graham.

Martha Graham is the high priestess of modern dance. She has created an entirely original style of dancing, a school of dance and a company. Several of the directors of important modern American dance companies, such as Merce Cunningham and Paul Taylor, were once dancers in her company. Her system has spread much further than America and can be seen in use in two of our British ballet companies (see pages 62 to 65).

What is the first thing that you will notice about Graham dance that is different from classical ballet? The costumes are much simpler: generally the leotard (a combined vest and trunks) replaces the classical *tutu*. Secondly, the dancers usually dance with bare feet.

The floor is the base to which the Graham dancer continually returns by means of falls and slides. This is one of the differences between classical and Graham dance, because the classical dancer tries to free himself from the ground, rising on his toes and leaping away from the floor. Every movement in Graham starts from the centre of the body, so that even a movement of the arms or legs emanates from there. This leads the Graham dancer to seek inside himself, so that a Graham-style ballet is often a ballet of ideas as well as of interesting movement.

Notation

It is a sad fact that many great ballets of the past are now lost for ever because there was no way of recording them. While a work can be handed on from one dancer to another it can continue to be presented even if the choreographer is no longer alive. But for centuries dancers have tried to devise some way of writing dances down so that they would not have to rely solely on their memories. A system of notation was invented as early as the sixteenth century but it wasn't until the present century that any were perfected and made practical.

One of the first of these was devised by a Russian, Vladimir Stepanov, and it was with the aid of his Stepanov notation that Nicolas Sergueff, ballet master of the Maryinsky Ballet from 1904 to 1917, was able to mount the first British versions of the classics. Although Stepanov's system was somewhat complicated to write down, Leonide Massine has successfully adapted it for his own use.

There are now two simpler systems in use, known as the Benesh and Laban systems. Of the two, the first is commonly used and several ballet companies have at least one Benesh notator to record the company's repertory. The Royal Ballet School teaches both the Benesh and Massine systems.

4. A Dancer's Day

To the outsider ballet appears a very glamorous profession. But if that is all that appeals to you about ballet, then my advice is: don't become a dancer. A dancer's life is hard. He works nearly every day of his active life, often from 10.00 in the morning until 10.00 at night, six days a week. Yet in his early forties a dancer must think about retiring: the only alternatives are staying in the company to perform character roles or taking up a teaching post.

Let us take a look at a typical day in the life of a dancer. The day begins with class, which generally runs from 10.00 until 11.30. Next comes a rehearsal and this may last well into the afternoon. Then there is the performance itself from 7.30 or 8.00 until 10.00 or even 10.30. If the dancer is in a touring company this will occur six nights a week with a midweek and a Saturday matinée. And, to top this, Sunday will probably be spent travelling.

Now let us consider a dancer's day in a little more detail.

Class

A dancer must practise nearly every day. In this way he keeps his muscles supple, his joints from becoming stiff; he retains his poise, grace and balance; he strengthens his technique. To that end he goes through a series of exercises in a studio. This is known as class.

There is a saying amongst dancers: if you miss class for one day, you know it; two days, your teacher knows it; three days and the audience knows it.

Class takes place in a ballet studio, which is usually a high, well-lit, large room with a wooden floor. If you are permitted to watch a company class this is what you will see. In one corner is a piano. Along at least one wall there is a continuous, floor to ceiling mirror. In front of this is the *barre*. This is a horizontal pole running the length of each wall, about three feet six inches from the floor.

The dancers assemble for the class. They will probably be dressed in either a leotard or a vest, and tights; but, in fact, anything goes. You may be surprised to see the legs of some of the dancers wrapped in thick woollen leggings. These are leg warmers and they help to keep the legs warm while the muscles are unexercised or during a break in the class.

Now class begins, with the piano for accompaniment. Class will be taken by the ballet master or mistress. If the company is large the men and women will have separate classes in different studios.

Class is divided into two main parts: the *barre* and centre practice. The exercises at the *barre* warm up the dancer's muscles and render the limbs strong and supple. They are done resting one hand on the *barre*, then repeated facing the opposite direction with the other hand on the *barre*.

The dancers move into the centre of the studio, suitably spaced out so that there is room for each to move freely. The exercises are now repeated without the support of the *barre*. Centre practice continues with *adage* (the slow movements) followed by *allegro* (the fast movements). Throughout the class the teacher will correct a dancer's execution of the given movements when necessary.

If the exercises were exactly the same every day there would be a danger that they would be performed too mechanically. So the teacher sets various combinations of steps (*enchaînements*). The *allegro* section will include various jumps, beaten steps (such as *entrechats*, in which one leg beats against the other) and turns in the exercises.

Men of the Kirov Ballet in centre practice during class

Rehearsal

After class there will probably be a rehearsal. This may take place in the studio or on stage. One occasion when the dancers must have the stage is for the dress rehearsal of a new or revived ballet. The dress rehearsal takes place shortly before the first night and the rehearsal will be a complete run through of the ballet with an orchestra, the stage being set and the dancers (or most of them) in costume. This is when photographers are allowed into the theatre to take pictures which will later appear in newspapers and magazines together with reviews of the ballet.

However, let us assume that today's rehearsal is of a ballet already in the repertory and that it is taking place in the studio. It is probable that the soloists will be running through their parts in one studio and the *corps de ballet* in another. The rehearsal will be taken by the ballet master or mistress or by the *répétiteur*, who is a member of the company responsible for teaching the ballets from memory. The company's artistic director may be present to watch and make comments. The music for the rehearsal will be supplied either by the piano or a tape.

The dancers will rehearse in the same assortment of clothes that they have already worn during class. What will strike you as very

Ekaterina Maximova
of the Bolshoi Ballet
tying the ribbons of her
ballet shoe during a rehearsal.
She is wearing a flimsy
practice skirt over her tights

strange is that they may hardly dance at all. The principals will walk about the studio making strange gestures with their hands, a look of intense concentration on their faces. What they are actually doing is indicating the steps they should be making. Or they may dance without dancing flat out. This is known as marking. If they were to dance full out after an exhausting class they would be too tired to give of their best at that evening's performance.

All this may appear like bedlam to the layman, yet out of this

Vladimir Vasiliev in the title role of the Bolshoi Ballet's *Spartacus*

A young student
practising Lise's mime
from act two of
La Fille mal gardée

Julia Farron
of the Royal Ballet
School teaching the
Lilac Fairy's mime
from *The Sleeping Beauty*

A classical class: the Royal Ballet in a special television studio class

A Graham class: students and dancers at The Place

Nadia Nerina and David Blair, the creators of Lise and Colas, in the first act of
Frederick Ashton's *La Fille mal gardée*

apparent chaos will come the finished performance that you will see in the evening.

However, if the rehearsal is for a new ballet the dancers will be dancing full out. They will try a sequence indicated by the choreographer. They will be asked to repeat certain sections if they are not right or if the choreographer wants to see how all the sections he has created so far look when linked together. There will be discussions between dancers and choreographer, possibly resulting in some slight changes. There may be disagreements about the timing if the dancer is unable to phrase a section at the required speed. All in all, there will be much trial and error.

Performance

The dancer will arrive at the theatre some time before the start of the evening performance. In the dressing room he may change into a dressing gown before applying his make-up and fitting his wig— though nowadays wigs are less common in ballet than they used to be. He then changes into his costume. The woman will put on her *pointe* shoes, the ribbons having been sewn in place and the blocked toes darned to make them last. The men's shoes have no ribbons to keep them from slipping off, so they are generally held in place by a piece of elastic across the arch of the foot, or, if the elastic will look unsightly, glue or spit is applied to the inside of the heel. To reduce the chances of slipping, the dancer will plant the flat of each foot into the shallow, square rosin box which is kept in the wings, working the foot from side to side to coat the sole and toe with the white powdered rosin.

Then he will find a space somewhere in the wings or on stage to warm up his muscles by exercising, because to go on stage cold could be disastrous, resulting in pulled or torn muscles. There will probably be time to practise some tricky steps from tonight's ballet

D

on stage either by himself or with his partner. Then the stage curtain comes down and the audience is admitted to the auditorium.

All the preparations are at an end. The curtain rises. The performance begins. The curtain comes down half an hour or so later on the first ballet or the first act of a full-length ballet. The dancer returns to the dressing room to change for the next ballet or act. This will probably entail a change of costume, wig and even make-up. The ballerina may change her shoes.

And so the evening continues through three or four ballets or acts. At the end comes the applause, the bouquets of flowers for the ballerina and soloists. The dancer changes back into his street clothes and, having looked at the call-board to see whether he will be required for tomorrow's rehearsals, departs through the stage door. There may be a small crowd of fans waiting, autographs to sign. Perhaps, muses the dancer, it's all worthwhile after all!

5. Taking up Ballet

So you want to take up ballet? If the answer is 'Yes', first take stock of yourself to see if you are suitable. Ideally you should be of medium height, slim and long-legged, and in good health. You will also need a sense of rhythm. And you mustn't be too old when you start your training. If you don't begin until your late teens you may never make the grade because your muscles will be too set and unable to take the strains of daily class and performance.

Teachers and Ballet Schools

If you conform to most or all of the above requirements then your first and most important step is to find yourself a teacher. You may find one near your home. Before enrolling, try to discover his or her qualifications. Has he any teaching certificates? Was he ever a dancer? Does he get good examination results from his students? Do the students often get accepted into ballet companies? If the answer to two or more of these questions is 'Yes' then enrol with that teacher.

If you are a girl you will be eager to start straight away dancing in *pointe* shoes. However, if you did, your feet and spine would probably be damaged, possibly permanently. So, train for at least two to three years in soft-toed shoes or flats. Normally you will be about thirteen before you begin to practise in blocked shoes.

Your teacher will probably be connected with one of the organ-
isations which arrange ballet examinations, such as the Royal
Academy of Dancing, the British Ballet Organisation or the Imperial Society of Teachers of Dancing. Once your training is under
way you will study for and take the various graded ballet examinations set by that organisation. Passing examinations doesn't auto-
matically qualify you for a place in a ballet company, but it does
show that you have reached a certain technical standard.

So far I have only told you about the private teacher. However,
you may wish to join one of the larger ballet schools, such as the
Royal Ballet School, Arts Educational, Bush Davies or Elmhurst
Schools, which combine a general education with the ballet
training.

The Royal Ballet School

There are between 125 and 130 pupils in the Junior School, which
is at White Lodge in the grounds of Richmond Park, Surrey. Com-
petition for entry to the School is very keen. Even the forty boys'
places are highly sought after at auditions. The lucky boys and
girls start at White Lodge at the age of eleven. The first year is a
trial period and from then on the student's progress is assessed
annually. The School provides for both day pupils and boarders.

At sixteen successful students transfer to the Upper School at
Talgarth Road in Baron's Court, London, where they are on
trial for the first three months. The students are put through their
final training and they may also continue to study English Language,
English Literature and French for Ordinary and Advanced Level
G.C.E. At eighteen they may be lucky enough to enter the parent
Royal Ballet company; if not, they will probably join one of the
other English or foreign ballet companies.

One of the highlights of the year for the students at both halves
of the School is the season at the Open Air Theatre in Holland

Park and the Theatre on the Green at Richmond, Surrey. Here the students will show their paces in both works from the Royal Ballet repertory and, generally, a piece created especially for them. However, *the* highlight of the year is the annual matinée at Covent Garden, where budding Seymours, Sibleys, Walls or Dowells can at last dance on the same boards as their illustrious seniors.

Joining a Company

Once you have reached professional standard you will want to join a company. You can write to the various British companies, but as there are not many places available at any one time, you may not be successful. If not, you can try one or more of the companies abroad. You will have to go for an audition, which usually entails taking part in a class. Unless you are extremely talented, don't expect to be accepted by the first company for which you audition. This may be a time of frustration and disappointment, but if you have talent and the real desire to dance then you should be lucky in finding a place somewhere.

6. British Ballet Today

The best way to learn about ballet is to see it for yourself. If you live in or near London this shouldn't be too difficult. In many ways London can be considered the capital city of ballet, for all the British companies appear there and all the important foreign ones come from time to time. But if you live outside London, do not despair; all the British companies tour the country, and you are sure to live near enough to some town where ballet is performed.

As well as performing different works, each company has a highly distinctive and individual personality. Let us take a closer look at the main British companies so that you will know just what type of ballet and what kind of programme you can expect to see.

The Royal Ballet

This is now the largest and most famous of the British companies. It has travelled as far afield as America, Russia and Japan. When it was formed in 1931 it had only seven dancers. Now there are more than 130, divided among three groups: the company at the Royal Opera House, a smaller touring group and *Ballet For All*.

(*Opposite*) Margot Fonteyn in the first act of *The Sleeping Beauty*

Symphonic Variations, with Gary Sherwood, Ann Jenner, Antoinette Sibley, Jennifer Penney and Anthony Dowell

Posing for a photograph on *The Grand Tour* the passengers include Noël Coward, Gertrude Lawrence, the American Lady (*seated centre*), Douglas Fairbanks lifting Mary Pickford, and Bernard Shaw (*far right*)

The Royal Ballet at Covent Garden

The Royal Opera House, Covent Garden, has been the home of the Royal Ballet since 1946. For much of the year the company gives several performances of ballet a week, the remainder of the week being given over to performances by the Royal Opera.

The basis of the company's repertory since the early days at Sadler's Wells has been the classics. Any large classical company of repute must have these as its foundation. It must also encourage the creation of new works to build up the repertory. This the Royal Ballet has done under three successive directors: Ninette de Valois, its founder, Frederick Ashton, and Kenneth MacMillan, the present director.

There are many fine dancers in the company, most of whom are seen to advantage in both contemporary works and the classics. A great number of them have received their training at the Royal Ballet School and so display what has become known as the British style of dancing.

What is this British style? It is reserved, as the British character is generally supposed to be. Our dancers are noted for their elegant line, their neat, quick footwork and for their lyricism—their poetry of movement. This lyricism is seen at its finest in the ballets of Frederick Ashton, undeniably the greatest British choreographer.

Ashton has created numerous ballets, most of them for the Royal Ballet. Much of his best work has been for Margot Fonteyn, for whom he has created, among other ballets, *Symphonic Variations*, *Daphnis and Chloë* and *Marguerite and Armand*, with Rudolf Nureyev, Fonteyn's famous partner, as Armand.

Although *Symphonic Variations* is no longer danced by Fonteyn, it still holds its own as one of Ashton's most perfect ballets. It is pure abstract dance. Against Sophie Fedorovitch's green setting decorated with flowing black lines, six dancers in white move to the melodies of César Franck's Symphonic Variations for piano and orchestra. To watch this sublime work is one of the most uplifting experiences that ballet can offer.

Two other Ashton ballets which you might like to see are *La Fille mal gardée* and *The Dream*. *La Fille mal gardée*, which is a pastoral ballet in two acts, is one of this choreographer's most delightful works. Its pleasures include a very funny dance by a cockerel and his hens; a brilliant cornfield *pas de deux* for the young lovers, Lise and Colas; and a hilarious clog dance for Lise's mother, Widow Simone (danced by a man). The ballet has witty designs by the cartoonist Osbert Lancaster and charming music by the nineteenth-century composer Hérold.

The Dream is a one-act ballet based on Shakespeare's *A Midsummer Night's Dream* and is danced to the well-known music by Mendelssohn. To condense the play into an hour-long ballet Ashton has had to make certain cuts, but he has managed to distil the essence of Shakespeare's play. So we can still revel in the confusion caused by the spells cast on the two pairs of lovers by the Fairy King Oberon and his nimble helper Puck; in Bottom transformed into an ass, prancing on his tiny hooves; and in proud Titania, the Fairy Queen, falling in love with this ridiculous creature. And *The Dream* is crowned by one of Ashton's loveliest creations, a *pas de deux* for the reconciled Oberon and Titania.

Another ballet in the company's repertory based on a play by Shakespeare is Kenneth MacMillan's *Romeo and Juliet*. The music was composed by the Russian Sergei Prokofiev and the first Soviet production for the Kirov had choreography by Leonide Lavrovsky. MacMillan uses the same score but has done new choreography to tell the story of the star-crossed lovers. This three-act ballet makes a spectacular and exciting evening, with its glittering ball, its colourful street scenes and its thrilling sword fights. It also has its more tender moments, notably in the passionate balcony *pas de deux* which closes the first act. The last act offers the dancer portraying Juliet the opportunity to display her acting ability in scenes of great emotional power.

The Royal Ballet does not appear only in ballets by British choreographers, but also in works by choreographers of other nationalities. There are several ballets by George Balanchine in the repertory, including two created for Diaghilev, *Apollo* and *The Prodigal Son*, and the more recent *Agon*, which is danced in black practice costume. An American whose ballets are danced by the company is Jerome Robbins. His *Dances at a Gathering* is a beautiful, witty and moving piece for a cast of ten, danced to Chopin played on the piano. It is just over an hour of sheer enchantment. Finally I must mention Glen Tetley, who has created two ballets, *Field Figures* and *Laborintus*, for the company using a technique combining classical and Graham dance and so extending the company's technical accomplishments.

The Royal Ballet New Group

Instead of performing large-scale works such as *Romeo and Juliet* or *Swan Lake*, which are best staged in an opera house, this touring group gives programmes of three or four one-act ballets for fairly small casts. These small-scale ballets are seen to much better advantage in the small theatres in which this group usually appears. Some of the ballets given by the group have been in the repertory of the Royal Ballet for many years. For instance, there is Frederick Ashton's *Les Patineurs*, Ninette de Valois' *The Rake's Progress* and John Cranko's *Pineapple Poll*.

Les Patineurs makes a sparkling start to any evening. As the title suggests, it is a skating ballet. It has no story but just shows people enjoying themselves—and occasionally coming to grief—on the ice. It builds up to an exciting climax with two girls performing spectacularly fast turns and a boy spinning like a top in the falling snow.

The Rake's Progress is a dramatic ballet based on the series of paintings by the eighteenth-century artist Hogarth. The rake is seen frittering away a fortune that he has inherited. In an attempt to pay back his debts he gambles, but loses his money and his reason. He dies in the asylum, mourned only by the inmates and a young girl that he had once betrayed.

For a piece in happier vein there is *Pineapple Poll*, danced to tunes from the Gilbert and Sullivan operas. The ballet is set at a port, both on land and on board Captain Belaye's ship. This gives the excuse for some jolly sailors' dances and a twinkling hornpipe from the Captain. In complete contrast there is a touching scene in which Jasper, the pot-boy at the inn who is in love with Poll, finds her clothes by the quayside and thinks that she has drowned herself. In reality Poll has fallen for the dashing Captain and dressed herself in sailor's clothes to get on board his ship. Go and see the ballet if you would like to know how the story resolves itself.

This group also performs ballets created especially for it. One of these is Joe Layton's *The Grand Tour* with the music (and singing voice) of Noël Coward. It is a charming and funny account of an American spinster on a sea cruise who comes into contact with celebrities of the 1930s, such as Mary Pickford, Douglas Fairbanks, Gertrude Lawrence and Noël Coward.

Ballet For All

Ballet For All tours extensively, visiting small theatres, civic halls and schools. To describe this group as the educational branch of the Royal Ballet would be correct, but might make it sound boring and stuffy. Far from it. *Ballet For All* is entertainment. It presents what it calls ballet-plays, in which speech, dancing and music are combined. These full-length ballet-plays tell audiences about the

Festival Ballet's *The Three Cornered Hat*, with Juan Sanchez and Noleen Nicol (*centre*) as the Miller and his wife. The striking set and costumes are by Picasso

Hilarion (Ashley Killar) and Berthe (Caroline Douglas) over the dead body of Giselle (Elaine McDonald) at the dramatic end to the first act of Scottish Theatre Ballet's *Giselle*

The bird
(Carol Barrett)
and the wolf
(Jonathan Thorpe)
in Northern
Dance Theatre's
Peter and the Wolf

Christopher Bruce
in the title role
of Ballet Rambert's
Pierrot Lunaire

art and history of ballet. For instance, *Two Coppélias* shows us what parts of *Coppélia* must have looked like when it was created in 1870, when the male lead was danced by a girl, and how it appears today.

Festival Ballet

The largest company after the Royal Ballet is Festival Ballet, or to give it its full title London Festival Ballet. It has a more popular appeal than the company at Covent Garden, and its audiences are drawn from a wide-ranging and less specialised public. Unlike the Royal Ballet, this company does not have a specifically British style because its dancers come from all over the world and it regularly invites the best international dancers as guest artists.

The company tours extensively. When in London it appears at both the New Victoria Theatre and the Coliseum, but it is most closely linked with the Royal Festival Hall on the South Bank of the Thames. However, the seasons at the Festival Hall are hampered by the wide yet shallow stage, and the company is seen to far better advantage at the London Coliseum in St Martin's Lane, one of the best theatres for ballet in the country.

Festival Ballet dances all the classics, in versions which differ from those given by the Royal Ballet, and its *Nutcracker* (the ballet is *not* called *The Nutcracker Suite*!) is performed regularly every Christmas in London. The repertory also includes some of Fokine's most famous ballets created for Diaghilev, including *Prince Igor*, *Schéhérazade* and *Petrushka*. The Polovtsian Dances from the opera *Prince Igor* are a thrilling series of dances by warriors and their captive slaves. *Schéhérazade*, with its exotically coloured designs by Léon Bakst, is another exciting ballet. It is set in a shah's harem and danced to the well-known music by Rimsky-Korsakov.

Petrushka is danced to Stravinsky's brilliant score. It is set in a fairground in old Russia at carnival time. Petrushka, the Ballerina and the Moor are three human-sized puppets brought to life by the showman. Grotesque Petrushka loves the silly Ballerina, but she prefers the clumsy Moor. Petrushka, a doll with human feelings, laments his fate. He breaks out of the cell where he is kept prisoner by the showman, and bursts in on the Ballerina and the Moor. The Moor chases Petrushka and kills him. The showman picks up the figure of Petrushka and shows it to the alarmed crowd: it is only a puppet filled with sawdust. But as night falls Petrushka's ghost appears to taunt the frightened showman.

Another Diaghilev ballet acquired by the company is Massine's *The Three Cornered Hat*. This work combines classical ballet and Spanish dancing in a manner which is unique in ballet. It has a rousing score by the Spanish Manuel de Falla and designs in strong lines and flat areas of colour by another Spaniard, Pablo Picasso. The role of the Miller, originally danced by Massine himself, offers the dancer a great challenge, particularly in the *farucca*, a brilliant and exciting solo.

Like the Royal Ballet, Festival Ballet has works by Balanchine in its repertory. These include *Night Shadow*, a romantic and dramatic piece using music from operas by Bellini. It tells of a poet who falls in love with a woman who walks in her sleep. The core of the ballet is a beautiful *pas de deux* in which the poet declares his love for the woman. In this he spins her around and gently pushes her so that she glides across the stage. Yet the woman is completely unaware of his presence because she is fast asleep.

Scottish Theatre Ballet

This company was originally based in the West of England, but in 1969 it changed its name from Western Theatre Ballet to Scottish

Theatre Ballet and moved to Glasgow to become Scotland's national ballet company. In some ways this company can be thought of as the link between the classical Royal and Festival Ballet, and the modern dance companies. The repertory is made up mainly of one-act ballets, of which a number have been choreographed by the company's director Peter Darrell. His ballets use classical technique but are modern in theme. His narrative ballets are not generally peopled by fairies, princes and princesses but by recognizable human beings faced by the problems of today.

However, Darrell has not entirely ignored the classics. Like both the Royal and Festival Ballet, Scottish Theatre Ballet performs several pieces by August Bournonville. The most famous is Bournonville's version of *La Sylphide*. It was created four years after the Taglioni version using a new score by Løvenskjold, and is still in the repertory of several companies, including the Royal Danish Ballet. The Taglioni version is now lost, but Bournonville's *La Sylphide*, like *Giselle*, remains as one of the great romantic ballets still regularly performed today.

Perhaps it is not surprising that the company should also have a version of *Giselle* in its repertory. However, this is a *Giselle* far removed from the usual treatment of the work. Darrell has set the ballet back into medieval times to underline the religious and superstitious elements in the story. He has made the characters seem real and believable for once, with Giselle and her mother part of the community of a small, walled town instead of living in the usual almost isolated cottage in the middle of a forest. The *wilis* of the second act are not the familiar pretty visions in tulle, but sinister harpies haunting the rocks. For a different view of this familiar ballet, I would recommend Scottish Theatre Ballet's version.

Northern Dance Theatre

Northern Dance Theatre was founded by Laverne Meyer, formerly a principal dancer of Western Theatre Ballet. Meyer, feeling that there was a need for a ballet company in the north-west of England, chose Manchester as its base.

This young company of about fifteen dancers appears in theatres, schools and civic halls. As well as works by Meyer himself, the repertory includes ballets by members of the company and outside choreographers.

A couple of the works performed by the company were once in the repertory of the old Ballet Rambert. One of these is Frank Staff's witty *Peter and the Wolf*. It is danced to the well-known music for children by Prokofiev. Peter, danced by a girl, has great fun catching the wicked wolf with the aid of a fluttering bird and a slinky cat, but only after the wolf has gobbled up the silly duck. 'If you listen very carefully, you can still hear the duck quacking inside the wolf; because in his hurry he'd swallowed her alive!'

Ballet Rambert

The Ballet Rambert today is a company presenting contemporary works using Graham as well as classical technique, so you may be surprised to know that once it performed ballets similar to those danced by the Royal Ballet. However, by 1966 Ballet Rambert was facing a financial crisis, so a smaller company of soloists only was formed. It preserved a few of the best of the short works from the past, and new and experimental ballets were created for it.

The new repertory has as its basis a number of ballets by Rambert's co-director, Norman Morrice, and includes several works by Glen Tetley. Members of the company are encouraged to create ballets, and one of the principal dancers, Christopher Bruce, has to date done six.

One of Norman Morrice's best ballets is undoubtably *Blind-Sight*, performed to a haunting jazz score by Bob Downes. Near the start all the dancers are huddled together like so many newborn kittens. These blind people explore their surroundings, inevitably blundering into the shimmering metal poles of Nadine Baylis' set. Gradually all but one regain their sight, but this leads to a violent ending to Morrice's gripping ballet.

You will, I'm sure, be intrigued by at least two of Tetley's ballets. *Pierrot Lunaire* is one of his earliest works. The characters in the ballet are those of the Italian *commedia dell'arte*, which flourished from the sixteenth to the eighteenth centuries and eventually gave rise in England to the characters of Punch and Harlequin. The three characters in Tetley's ballet are Pierrot, Columbine and Brighella. Innocent Pierrot, for ever catching moonbeams, is teased and tormented by Columbine and Brighella, but at the ballet's moving close forgives them both.

Ziggurat—the Ziggurat being an Assyrian temple-tower—has strange, primeval men who encounter a god-like creature and angelic women in white. The score by Karlheinz Stockhausen and the beautiful projections help to make this a really magical piece.

I hope you'll like Linda Hodes' *The Act*, in which a life-size dummy in a cabaret act rebels against his master and finally changes place with him. I must also mention *'Tis Goodly Sport*, a ballet created by Jonathan Taylor, which is a lively and very funny piece to early English music.

The company also appears in theatres such as London's Young Vic and Sheffield's Crucible Theatre, which have thrust stages. In these the dancers are enclosed on three sides by the audience. Thrust stages demand an entirely new approach to ballet making, and to that end a number of ballets have been specially created for them. These include John Chesworth's *Pattern for an Escalator* and Christopher Bruce's *There Was a Time*, based on the Trojan war.

London Contemporary Dance Theatre

The London home of this modern group is The Place, a converted Army Drill Hall near Euston Station. Most members of the company have received their training at the London School of Contemporary Dance, also housed at The Place. The School, which was set up in 1966, is the only one in Europe which Martha Graham permits to teach her technique. The director of the company, Robert Cohan, was for a number of years a dancer in Martha Graham's company and the choreography of many of the works performed by the Dance Theatre is by him. The repertory also includes ballets by past and present members of the company, such as William Louther and Robert North, and works by outside choreographers.

Like Martha Graham's company, London Contemporary Dance Theatre performs many works using mythical and biblical themes. For instance, Barry Moreland's *Kontakion* is based on the life of Christ and Cohan's *Hunter of Angels* on the Old Testament story of the struggle between Jacob and the Angel.

The rest of the works are more difficult to classify. Most are intended for small casts—as the company only consists of about fifteen dancers—and are highly experimental. Some of the pieces will make you think. As I have already explained, this is because modern dance is concerned not only with interesting movement but also with ideas. However, as with much modern art, these may not be expressed directly and it will be up to you to seek out a meaning. This may not be the meaning that the choreographer had in mind, but it will probably be just as valid.

Not all modern ballets have such serious intentions. Some can

Paul Taras with Dreas Reyneke (*behind*) in Ballet Rambert's *Ziggurat*

Zany modern dance: London Contemporary Dance Theatre in *Three Epitaphs*

An imaginative ballet film: Norman McLaren's *Pas de Deux*

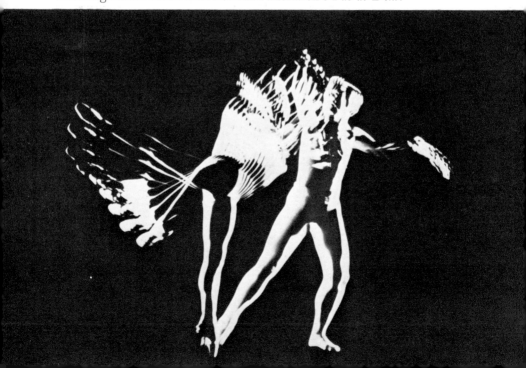

even make you laugh. In *Three Epitaphs* by Paul Taylor, the amiable giant of American modern dance, there are five creatures clad in brown from head to toe, with pieces of mirror on their heads and the palms of their hands. They lope about, their arms hanging ape-like at their sides until galvanized into sudden whirling movements. They are rather slow-witted and have a tendency to bump into one another. The impression made by these inhuman creatures with human characteristics is both weird and funny.

E

7. Ballet on the Screen

Cinema

Once a ballet performance is over all that is left is the memory of
the piece and the dancing in it. But, thanks to the cinema, there is a
method of preserving that performance on celluloid for all time.
So it is possible for you to watch Pavlova years after her death in
some of her most famous dances, including *The Dying Swan*. You
can also see many other famous dancers on film, such as Ulanova,
Plisetskaya and Fonteyn, even if you haven't been lucky enough
to see them on stage.

These films are either photographed stage performances or
productions set up in a studio and shot there. For instance, the
Bolshoi Ballet film of *Giselle* with Ulanova was recorded at Covent
Garden after an actual performance, whereas the film of *Don
Quixote*, based on the Australian Ballet's production, was made in
three aircraft hangars converted into film studios.

Once inside a studio it should be possible to create a ballet
especially for the medium. This would mean creating new dances
and devising them in terms of the cinema screen. Yet when this
happens the result is often disappointing.

The best original ballet or dance sequences are often those in
film musicals, such as *Seven Brides for Seven Brothers*, or the Fred

Astaire or Gene Kelly musicals. However, for the most imaginative use of dance in cinema musicals we must go right back to the nineteen thirties to the films of Busby Berkeley. His aerial shots of chorus girls, looking just like patterns in a colossal kaleidoscope, have never been surpassed.

Those are some aspects of filmed dance. However, the cinema is an art form in itself, so it ought to be possible to produce a ballet film that exists as an imaginative work of art in its own right. Yet, amazingly, I can think of only one such film. It is a short called *Pas de Deux*, filmed by the Scottish-Canadian Norman McLaren. You have probably seen those photographs which show the various stages of an action all on the one print. This is produced by simply opening the camera shutter many times without moving on the film. Now imagine a film of two dancers in movement, with each frame looking like one of those photographs, and you will have some idea of Norman McLaren's film. (You can see a still from the film opposite page 65.) It may not look much like traditional ballet, but it gives us an entirely new awareness of movement.

Television

It is highly probable that before you ever experienced any ballet in the theatre you had seen ballet on television. This will have given you some idea of what to expect in the theatre. Unfortunately, ballet on television is only a poor substitute for the real thing; the tiny image, probably in black and white, on the TV screen is almost always disappointing.

There are three types of television ballet. Firstly, there is the complete ballet photographed on stage or in the studio; secondly, the ballet extract—some *pas de deux* or other shown out of context; thirdly, the ballet created especially for television. The latter is extremely important because so much can be done in the medium that would be impossible on stage. However, as yet, television has attracted very few British choreographers. So we must look to Europe for creative television ballets, to Birgit Cullberg in Sweden and Flemming Flindt in Denmark. Fortunately their works do appear on British screens from time to time.

There is yet another approach to ballet on television, and that is the documentary. This will take you behind the scenes and show the hard work that goes into making a ballet, probably coupled with interviews with some of those concerned in its creation. This usually makes absorbing viewing. In this genre there was an American TV film which showed how New York City Ballet's Edward Villella worked himself to the point of exhaustion. In happier vein the BBC's programme showing the Royal Ballet in a special television studio class was one of the best ballet programmes that I've seen on the small screen.

Reading List

Books

This can only be a very small selection from the large number of books published on ballet. Some of these are now out of print but they should be available from either your library or a good second-hand bookshop. Books marked with an asterisk were still in print in January 1974.

Ballet For All, Peter Brinson and Clement Crisp (David and Charles —hardback; Pan—paperback)
> Over 100 ballets are described and discussed in detail. Peter Brinson was the founder of the Royal Ballet's *Ballet For All*.

Beginners, Please!, Kay Ambrose (A. & C. Black)
> A concentrated primer for ballet students of all ages.

The Complete Book of Ballets, C. W. Beaumont (Putnam)
> Not 'complete'—what book could be?—but together with its three supplementary volumes, it is a hefty work of reference by the doyen of British ballet writers.

The Dance Encyclopedia, Anatole Chujoy and P. W. Manchester (Simon and Schuster)
> Over 5,000 entries in this American encyclopedia.

The Diaghilev Balet 1909–1929, S. L. Grigoriev (Constable)
*Nijinsky, Romola Nijinsky (Sphere paperback)
*Nijinsky, Richard Buckle (Weidenfeld and Nicolson)
> For preference these three books should be read in conjunction. The first is an excellent history of this great company by its manager. The second is a biography of Nijinsky by his wife. The last is a very thorough book, which, apart from correcting some of the errors in the other two, supplies much new information on this dancer.

*A Dictionary of Ballet Terms, Leo Kersley and Janet Sinclair (A. & C. Black)
> A useful reference book which describes and illustrates those difficult technical terms.

*Era of the Russian Ballet 1770–1965, Natalia Roslavleva (Gollancz)
> Packed with facts, many otherwise unavailable. Profusely illustrated.

*A History of Ballet and its Makers, Joan Lawson (Dance Books)
> An excellent history of ballet.

*The Romantic Ballet in Paris, Ivor Guest (Pitman)
> A thorough account of the subject. Well illustrated.

The Sadler's Wells Ballet, Mary Clarke (A. & C. Black)
> A very good history of the present Royal Ballet from its beginnings until 1955. Unfortunately there is no one book which brings this up to date.

*Braunsweg's Ballet Scandals: The Life of an Impresario and the Story of Festival Ballet, Julian Braunsweg (George Allen and Unwin)
> After all those serious works, it's a delight to turn to this funny backstage account of the running of a ballet company.

Lastly, a very special book, Boris Kochno's *Le Ballet* (Hachette). The text, which covers the history of ballet, is in French. However, the illustrations are some of the largest and finest available in any book and include a particularly splendid section on the Diaghilev company. Unfortunately this book is scarce, which means that copies are expensive. However, there is a copy in the excellent Pavlova Memorial Library section of London's Westminster Reference Library, just off Leicester Square.

Magazines

In Britain there are two monthly magazines published on ballet, *Dance and Dancers* and *Dancing Times*. Both have articles and reviews on ballet at home and abroad, and the latter also covers the various ballet schools in some detail. Additionally, if you go regularly to Covent Garden, I would highly recommend *About the House*, the magazine of the Friends of Covent Garden, which has excellent articles and photographs on ballet and opera at Covent Garden. It appears four times a year and is obtainable from the Opera House.

Index

abstract ballet, *see* plotless ballet
Act, The, 63
adage, 29, 46
Adam, Adolphe, 27
Agon, 57
Alhambra Theatre, 34
allegro, 46, 47
American Ballet Theatre, 35
Apollo, 57
Après-midi d'un faune, L', 33
arabesque, 37
Arts Educational Schools, The, 52
Ashton, Frederick, 20, 55, 56, 57
Astaire, Fred, 66
attitude, 38
audition, 53
Australian Ballet, 34, 66

Bakst, Léon, 59
Balanchine, George, 33-4, 35, 57, 60
ballerina, 17, 23, 28-9, 41, 50
Ballet Comique de la Reine, 25
ballet d'action, 26
Ballet For All, see Royal Ballet
ballet master, 31, 32, 46, 48

Ballet Rambert, 20, 21, 34, 62-4
Ballet Royal de la Nuit, Le, 25
ballet studio, 45, 46, 47, 48
barre, 46
Bayadère, La, 29
Baylis, Nadine, 63
beaten steps, 26, 47
Béjart, Maurice, 35
Bellini, Vincenzo, 60
Berkeley, Busby, 67
Black Swan *pas de deux*, 32, 40, 42
Blind-Sight, 63
Bologna, Giovanni da, 38
Bolshoi Ballet, 17, 33, 35, 66
Bournonville, August, 35, 61
bourrée, 38-9
Brian, 20
British Ballet Organisation, The, 52
Bruce, Christopher, 21, 63, 64
Bush Davies Schools, 52

cabriole, 39
Camargo, Marie-Anne Cupis de, 26
Cantabile, 20
Capab Ballet, 34

Catherine de' Medici, 25
centre practice, 46
character dancer, 18, 23
Chesworth, John, 64
Chopin, Frederic, 57
choreographer, 18–20
Cinderella, 41
cinema ballet, 66–7
class, 45–7, 48, 53, 68
coda, 29, 40
Cohan, Robert, 64
Coliseum, London, 59
commedia dell'arte, 63
Coppélia, 59
Corelli, Jean, 27
corps de ballet, 18, 28–9, 48
court ballet, 25, 37
Covent Garden, *see* Royal Opera
    House, Covent Garden
Cranko, John, 34, 57
Crucible Theatre, Sheffield, 63
Cullberg, Birgit, 68
Cunningham, Merce, 43

Dances at a Gathering, 19, 57
danseur noble, 17–18
Daphnis and Chloë, 55
Darrell, Peter, 61
demi-caractère dancer, 18
design, 21–2
Diaghilev, Serge, 32–4, 35, 57, 59, 60
Diaghilev's Russian Ballet, 33–4
divertissement, 29, 30
Dolin, Anton, 34
Don Quixote, 66
Downes, Bob, 63
Dream, The, 56

Dying Swan, The, 33, 66

Elmhurst Ballet School, 52
Elssler, Fanny, 28
enchaînements, 46
entrechat, 40, 47

Falla, Manuel de, 60
farucca, 60
Fedorovitch, Sophie, 55
Festival Ballet, London, 34, 59–60, 61
Field Figures, 57
Field, John, 34
Fille mal gardée, La, 20, 56
Firebird, The, 33
five positions, 37
flats (soft shoes), 49, 51
Flindt, Flemming, 68
Flying Mercury, The, 38
Fokine, Michel, 32, 33, 35, 41, 59
Fonteyn, Margot, 17, 55, 66
For these who die as cattle, 21
fouetté, 40–1
Franca, Celia, 34
Franck, César, 56

Gala performance, 23
G.C.E. O. Level Ballet, 36
Gilbert and Sullivan, 58
Giselle, 18, 27–8, 34, 61, 66
Graham Company, 43, 64
Graham, Martha, 43, 64
Graham technique, 43, 57, 62, 64
Grand pas de deux, 30
Grisi, Carlotta, 27

Helpmann, Robert, 34

Henri II, 25
Hérold, Ferdinand, 56
Hodes, Linda, 63
Hogarth, William, 63
hornpipe, 58
Hunter of Angels, 64

Imperial Society of Teachers of
    Dancing, 52
Imperial Theatres, 32, 33
Ivanov, Lev, 31–2

jeté, 41
Jeux, 33
Joffrey Ballet, 35
joining a company, 53
jumps, 26, 47

Karsavina, Tamara, 33, 34
Kelly, Gene, 67
Kirov Ballet, 33, 35, 56
Kontakion, 64

Laborintus, 57
Lancaster, Osbert, 56
Lapzeson, Naomi, 20
Lavrovsky, Leonide, 56
Legnani, Pierina, 41
leg warmers, 46
leotard, 43, 46
Letters on the Dance, 26
Lifar, Serge, 34
lighting, 22
line, 29, 55
Living Space, 21
London Contemporary Dance Theatre,
    20, 64–5

London School of Contemporary
    Dance, 64
Louis XIV, 25, 37
Louther, William, 64
Løvenskjold, Herman, 61
lyricism, 55

MacMillan, Kenneth, 21, 55, 56
Mahler, Gustav, 21
make-up, 18, 49, 50
Marguerite and Armand, 55
marking, 48
Markova, Alicia, 34, 35
Maryinsky Ballet, 33, 35, 44
Maryinsky Theatre, 30, 31, 32
Massine, Leonide, 33, 44, 60
McLaren, Norman, 67
Mendelssohn-Bartholdy, Felix, 56
Meyer, Laverne, 62
Midsummer Night's Dream, A, 56
mime, 17, 18, 29, 32
modern dance, 42–3
Moreland, Barry, 64
Morrice, Norman, 62, 63
Morris dancers, 15
music, 20–1

narrative ballet, 19, 21
National Ballet of Canada, 34
New Victoria Theatre, 59
New York City Ballet, 35, 68
Night Shadow, 60
Nijinska, Bronislava, 21, 33
Nijinsky, Vaslav, 18, 33, 40
Noces, Les, 21
North, Robert, 20, 64
Northern Dance Theatre, 62

notation, 43–4
Noverre, Jean Georges, 26, 32
Nureyev, Rudolf, 18, 29, 55
Nutcracker, The, 31, 59
Nutcracker Suite, The, 59

Open Air Theatre, Holland Park, 52–3
Opéra, Paris, 34
Opus '65, 20

pas de deux, 29, 30, 31, 32, 40, 42, 56,
    57, 60, 67
Pas de Deux (film), 67
Patineurs, Les, 57–8
Pavillion d'Armide, Le, 33
Pavlova, Anna, 33, 66
performance, 49–50
Perrot, Jules, 27
Peter and the Wolf, 21, 62
Petipa, Marius, 28–30, 31, 32
Petit, Roland, 35
Petrushka, 33, 59–60
Picasso, Pablo, 21, 60
Pierrot Lunaire, 63
Pineapple Poll, 57, 58
pirouette, 42
Place, The, 64
plié, 36
Plisetskaya, Maya, 17, 18, 66
plotless ballet, 19, 21
pointe, 27
pointe shoes, 27, 49, 50, 51
Poole, David, 34
ports de bras, 37
Praagh, Peggy van, 34
Prince Igor, 59
Prodigal Son, The, 57

Prokofiev, Sergei, 56, 62

Rake's Progress, The, 57, 58
Rambert, Marie, 34
Raymonda, 29
rehearsal, 47–9
Reisinger, Wenzel, 31
répétiteur, 48
Rimsky-Korsakov, Nikolai, 59
Rite of Spring, The, 33
Robbins, Jerome, 19, 57
romantic ballet, 27–8
Romeo and Juliet, 56–7
Rose Adagio, 30
rosin, 49
Royal Academy of Dancing, The, 52
Royal Ballet, The, 21, 29, 34, 53, 54–9,
    60, 61, 62, 68
  at Covent Garden, 55–7
  Ballet For All, 58–9
  New Group, 57–8
Royal Ballet School, The, 44, 52–3, 55
Royal Danish Ballet, 35, 61
Royal Festival Hall, 59
Royal Opera, 55
Royal Opera House, Covent Garden,
    15, 23, 55, 59, 66
Russian dancers, concert items by, 23

Sacre du Printemps, Le, see *Rite of
    Spring*
Sadler's Wells Theatre, 55
Sallé, Marie, 26
Schéhérazade, 59
Scottish Theatre Ballet, 60–1
Serguéeff, Nicolas, 44
Seven Brides for Seven Brothers, 66

Shakespeare, William, 56
Sleeping Beauty, The, 17, 29, 30, 34
Sleeping Princess, The, see *Sleeping Beauty*
Sokolow, Anna, 20
Soloviev, Yuri, 18
Somes, Michael, 18
Song of the Earth, The, 21
Spectre de la Rose, Le, 33
Staff, Frank, 21, 62
Stepanov, Vladimir, 44
Stockhausen, Karlheinz, 63
Stravinsky, Igor, 21, 30, 33, 59
Sun King, The, see Louis XIV
Swan Lake, 17, 18, 31–2, 40, 57
Sylphide, La, 27, 33, 61
Sylphides, Les, 33
Symphonic Variations, 55–6

Taglioni, Filippo, 27, 61
Taglioni, Marie, 27
Taylor, Jonathan, 63
Taylor, Paul, 43, 65
Tchaikovsky, Peter, 30–1
teachers, 51–2
technique, 16–17, 36–44
television ballet, 67–8
Tetley, Glen, 21, 57, 62, 63
Theatre on the Green, Richmond, 53
There Was a Time, 64

Three Cornered Hat, The, 60
Three Epitaphs, 65
'Tis Goodly Sport, 63
tour en l'air, 42
Triumph of Love, The, 26
turnout, 36
turns, 42, 47
tutu, 29, 32, 43
Two Coppélias, 59
Tyl Eulenspiegel, 33

Ulanova, Galina, 66

Valois, Ninette de, 34, 55, 57
Vasiliev, Vladimir, 18
Vestris, Auguste, 26, 27
Vic-Wells Ballet, see Royal Ballet
Villella, Edward, 68

warm up, 49
Western Theatre Ballet, 60, 62
 see also Scottish Theatre Ballet
wig, 49, 50
Woizikowski, Leon, 34
World of Art, 32

Young Vic, The, 63

Ziggurat, 63